GEOLOGY ROCKS!

EARTH'S LAYERS

IZZI HOWELL

Please visit our website, www.garethstevens.com. For a free color catalog of all our high-quality books, call toll free 1-800-542-2595 or fax 1-877-542-2596.

Published in 2025 by
Gareth Stevens Publishing
2544 Clinton St.
Buffalo, NY 14224

First published in Great Britain in 2023 by Wayland

BE CAREFUL!

- Wear an apron and cover surfaces.
- Tie back long hair.
- Ask an adult for help with cutting.
- Check materials for allergens.

We recommend adult supervision at all times while doing the activities in this book. Always be aware that materials may contain allergens, so check the packaging for allergens if there is a risk of an allergic reaction. Anyone with a known allergy must avoid these.

Author and editor:
Izzi Howell

Series designer:
Rocket Design (East Anglia) Ltd

Proofreader:
Annabel Savery

Cataloging-in-Publication Data
Title: Earth's layers / Izzi Howell.
Description: Buffalo, NY : Gareth Stevens Publishing, 2025. | Series: Geology rocks! | Includes glossary and index.
Identifiers: ISBN 9781538293904 (pbk.) | ISBN 9781538293911 (library bound) | ISBN 9781538293928 (ebook)
Subjects: LCSH: Earth (Planet)--Core--Juvenile literature. | Earth (Planet)--Crust--Juvenile literature. | Earth (Planet)--Mantle--Juvenile literature.
Classification: LCC QE509.2 H68 2025 | DDC 551.1--dc23

Picture acknowledgements: Shutterstock: CRStocker cover top, title page, 3t, 8, 10tl, 12t and14t, VectorShow cover bottom left, Perfect_kebab cover bottom right, 24t and 32b, Virinaflora 2, Diego Barucco 3c and 26t, www.sandatlas.org 3b and 25, Sakurra 4, Sailorr 5t and 30t, tanyabosyk 5b, GoodStudio 6t, Volha Kratkouskaya and HappyPictures 6b, macrowildlife 7t, 28tr and 32t, honglouwawa 7b, everything bagel 9t and 10b, Vixit 9c, 3000ad 9b and 28tl, pizzastereo 10tr, BlueRingMedia 11t, Denis Belitsky 11b and 28cr, Alexander Lysenko and Ziablik 12c, vivat and Platon Anton 12b, VectorMine 13, VectorMine 14b, Peter Hermes Furian 15t, Tsekhmister 15b, Macrovector 16l, Designua 16–17c, Arunna 17 and 30b, EreborMountain 18 and 19, Nsit 20, Alena Kozlova 21t, Darryl Brooks 21b and 28cl, zombiu26 22t, GoodStudio 22b, trekandshoot 23 and 28br, Creativa Images 24b, tinkivinki 26b, Catmando 27, Bibadash 31t, ProStockStudio 31b.

All additional design elements from Shutterstock or drawn by designer.

Printed in the United States of America

CPSIA compliance information: Batch #CSGS25: For further information contact Gareth Stevens at 1-800-542-2595.

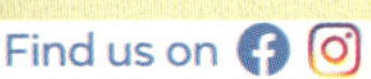

CONTENTS

Pressure affects conditions in the inner core. See page 8.

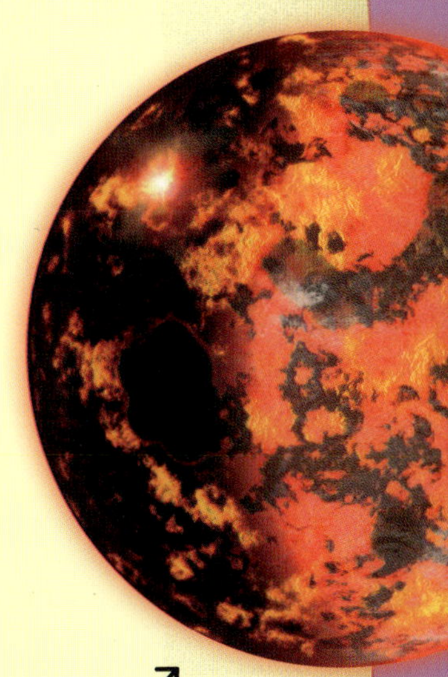

Earth used to look very different! Find out more on page 26.

What is a xenolith? Find out on page 25.

EARTH'S STRUCTURE

Earth is made up of four main layers.

Planet Earth is a massive sphere made of rock and metal. It is divided into four layers that lie at different depths beneath the surface.

The crust

The outer layer of Earth is called the crust. This is the layer that we live on. The crust is the thinnest layer. Find out more about the crust on pages 14-15.

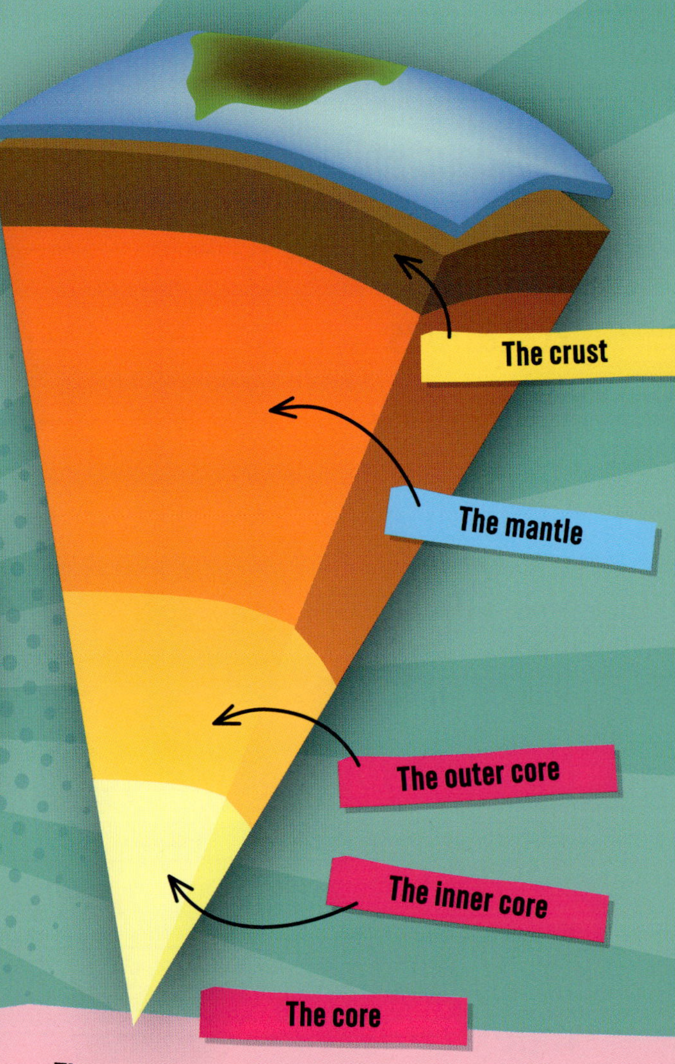

The mantle

The mantle lies beneath the crust. At about 1,800 miles (2,900 km) thick, it's the thickest of Earth's layers. Find out more about the mantle on pages 12–13.

The core

The core is found beneath the mantle. It is split into two sections—the outer core and the inner core. The inner core lies at the very center of Earth. Find out more about the outer core on pages 10–11 and the inner core on pages 8–9.

Earth is spherical, but it isn't perfectly round! It actually has a bit of a bulge around the middle and is slightly flattened at the poles.

Make a model of Earth's layers

You will need four different colors of modeling clay, a rolling pin, dental floss, and an adult to supervise.

1. Form a ball using one color of modeling clay. This represents Earth's inner core.

2. Roll out a circle of another color of modeling clay. Wrap it around the first ball and join the edges together so that the ball is totally covered. This layer represents the outer core.

3. Repeat step 2 twice with the other colors of modeling clay. These layers represent the mantle and the crust. If you want to make your model realistic, the final layer of the ball (crust) should be much thinner than the others.

4. Cut through the center of the ball using the dental floss to reveal a cross-section of Earth's layers! Try not to press down too hard so that you don't squish the layers.

EARTH'S MATERIALS

Earth is a rocky planet. It contains different minerals and metals, made from different elements.

Many different materials are found in Earth's layers.

We dig rock out of Earth's crust in quarries and mines.

What is a rock?

Rocks are made of different grains of minerals joined together. For example, the rock limestone is made out of the minerals calcite and aragonite. A mineral is a naturally occurring substance that does not come from plants or animals. Minerals are made up of different elements (the most basic substances on Earth). For example, calcite contains calcium, carbon, and oxygen.

What is a metal?

Some of the minerals found in rocks contain metals. A metal is a material that conducts heat and electricity, is typically shiny, and is usually solid at room temperature. Metals can be elements, like iron, or a mixture of different elements, like brass, which is made from copper and zinc.

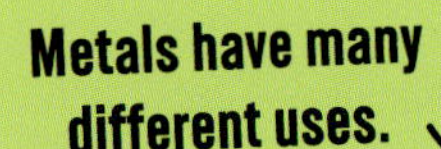

Metals have many different uses.

PHOTO QUIZ!

This metal is very valuable. What is it? Answer on page 28.

I'm so shiny!

Did you know?

A rock that contains metal is known as an ore.

The elements

More than 90 percent of planet Earth is made up of just four elements: iron, oxygen, silicon, and magnesium. There are also smaller amounts of other elements, such as nickel. Different elements are found in different layers. For example, most of the iron is in the core, while silicon and magnesium are found in the mantle and crust. Oxygen makes up nearly half of Earth's crust.

THE INNER CORE

The inner core is a solid ball at the center of Earth.

The inner core is very hot and very dense with very high pressure pressing inwards.

Heat and pressure

The inner core is the hottest layer. The temperature there is around 9,400°F (5,200°C). The very high pressure is caused by the weight of the rest of Earth's layers and Earth's atmosphere pushing inwards.

Melting mystery

The inner core is mostly made up of iron, with smaller amounts of nickel and sulfur. It is easily hot enough there for the iron to melt, but the inner core remains solid! Why? The answer is the inner core's very high pressure, which stops the iron from melting.

It's a fact

The diameter of the inner core is about 1,490 miles (2,400 km). That's about 250 times the height of Mount Everest!

PHOTO QUIZ!

Earth isn't the only planet with a metal core. All the planets have them! Which planet is this? Answer on page 28.

THE OUTER CORE

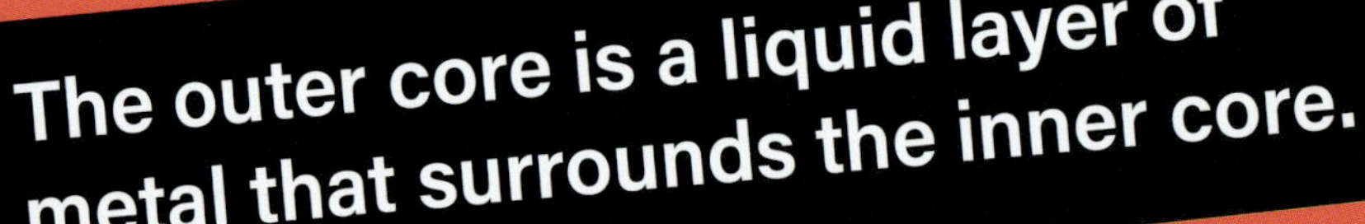

The outer core is a liquid layer of metal that surrounds the inner core.

The outer core is around 1,430 miles (2,300 km) thick. It's cooler than the inner core at around 7,230 to 9,030°F (4,000 to 5,000°C), but it's still pretty hot!

Liquid iron

Like the inner core, the outer core is also composed of iron, nickel, and sulfur. However, unlike the inner core, the iron here is in a liquid state, even though the temperature is cooler. This is because there is less pressure here than in the outer core.

Did you know?

The border between the inner and outer core is as hot as the surface of the sun!

Metal and magnets

Movement of liquid metal in the outer core creates Earth's magnetic field. This is a massive area around Earth with a magnetic force. Earth's magnetic field covers the whole of the planet and stretches out for many thousands of miles into space. It protects Earth from dangerous particles that come from the sun.

EARTH'S MAGNETIC FIELD

PHOTO QUIZ!

These beautiful lights, known as an aurora, happen when Earth's magnetic field pulls in some of the particles released by the sun. Where on Earth can you see them? Answer on page 28.

THE MANTLE

The mantle is the thickest layer.

The mantle is the middle layer inside Earth, lying between the outer core and the crust. It is mostly solid.

Mega mantle

The mantle is around 1,800 miles (2,900 km) deep. That's the distance between Chicago, Illinois, and Los Angeles, California! This makes it the largest of Earth's layers.

CHICAGO

LOS ANGELES

How far?!

It's a fact

The mantle makes up about 84 percent of Earth's total volume!

Hot and cold

The deeper into the mantle you go, the higher the temperature and pressure. The very hot inner and outer cores heat the rock in the mantle from below. The deeper areas of the mantle are very hot, but it's cooler near the crust.

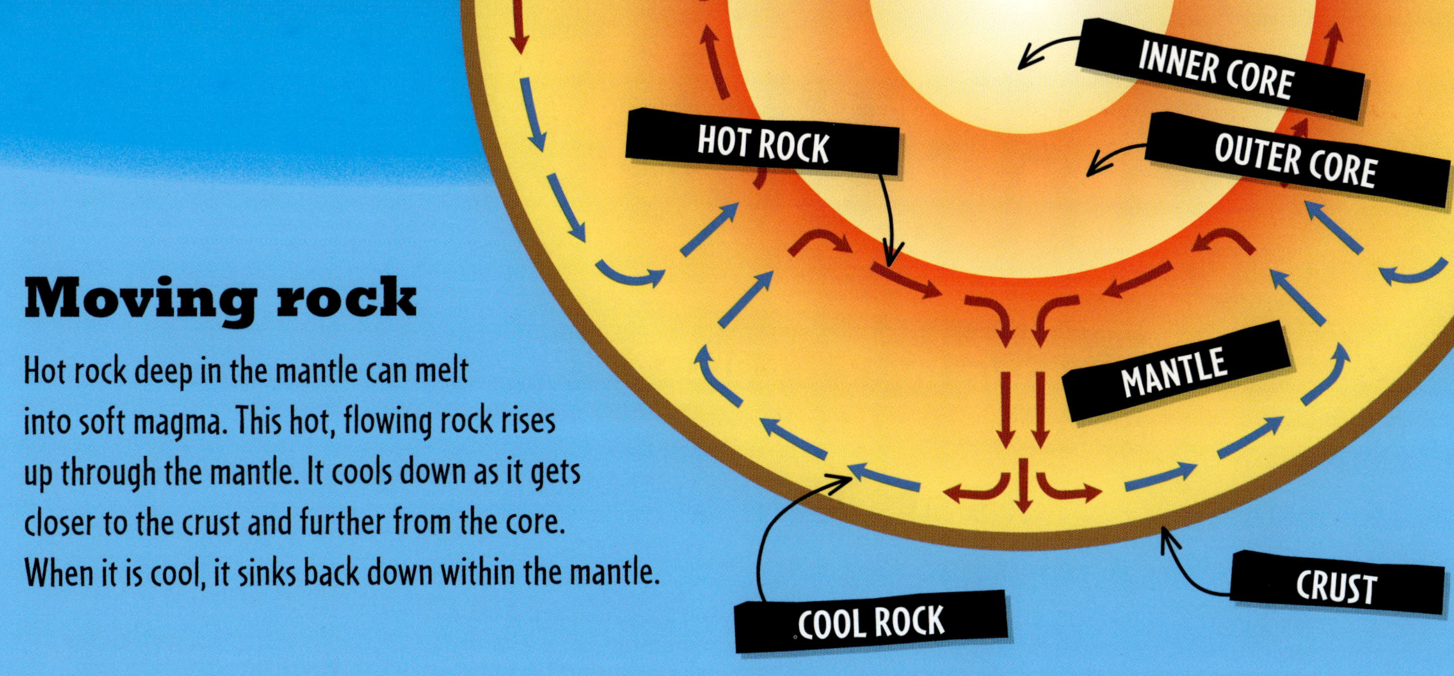

Moving rock

Hot rock deep in the mantle can melt into soft magma. This hot, flowing rock rises up through the mantle. It cools down as it gets closer to the crust and further from the core. When it is cool, it sinks back down within the mantle.

See how magma moves

You will need food coloring, water, a glass or clear jar, an ice cube tray, access to a freezer, and an adult's help.

1. Add food coloring drop by drop to a small amount of water until the water has a dark color.

2. Pour the colored water into an ice cube tray. Place in the freezer and leave overnight until frozen.

3. Fill the glass with warm water. Add one ice cube.

4. Watch what happens!

The ice cube melts in the warm clear water, releasing cold, colored water. The cold, colored water sinks to the bottom of the glass, pushing the warm, clear water up towards the top. This is exactly what happens in the mantle. Cool magma sinks to the bottom, pushing warm magma up towards the crust.

THE CRUST

We live on Earth's crust.

The crust is Earth's outer layer. It includes the surface that we live on, tall mountains, and the seabed beneath the oceans, as well as some rock beneath the surface that we can't easily see. There are two types of crust: oceanic and continental.

Under the sea

Oceanic crust is found under Earth's oceans and seas. It is about 3 to 6 miles (5 to 10 km) thick, which is thinner than continental crust. Oceanic crust is mostly made of an igneous rock called basalt. This comes up from the mantle in certain places (see page 19).

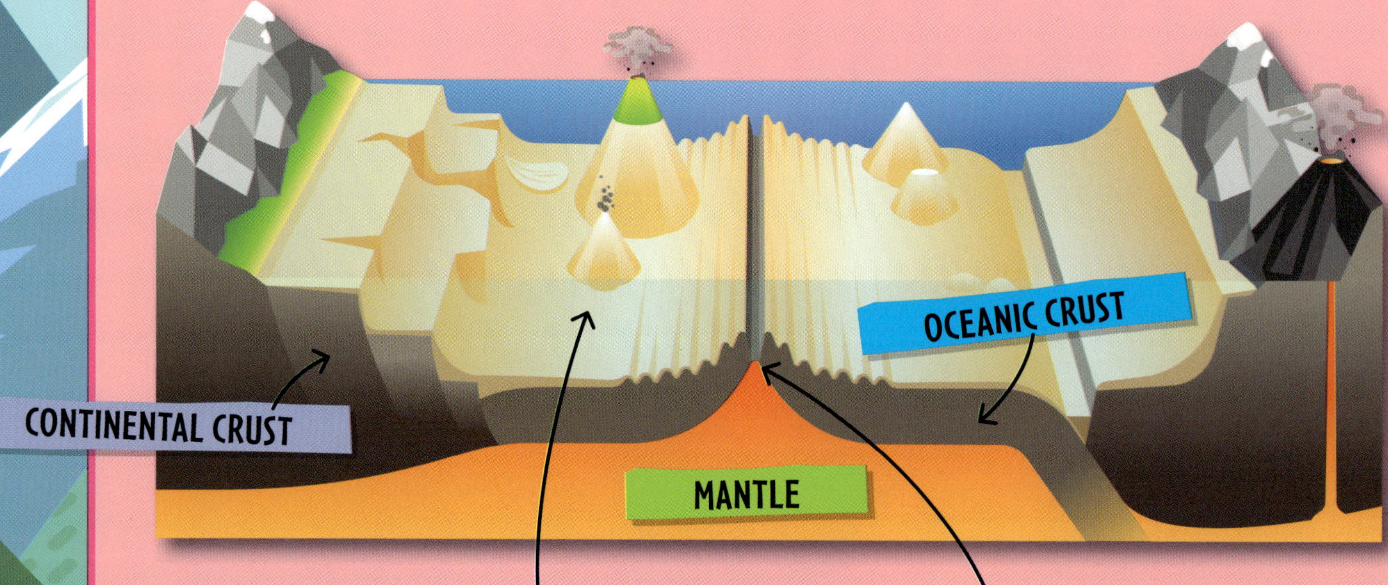

We can't easily see oceanic crust since it's at the bottom of the ocean. But it is as varied as the land we live on, with hills, mountains, and valleys.

Magma rises to the surface to create new oceanic crust. Find out more on page 19.

Feeling continental

Continental crust can be up to 43 miles (70 km) thick. It makes up the land in Earth's continents, as well as the seabed near the shore. Many different types of granite rock are found in the continental crust.

The land on Earth is divided into seven main areas, known as continents.

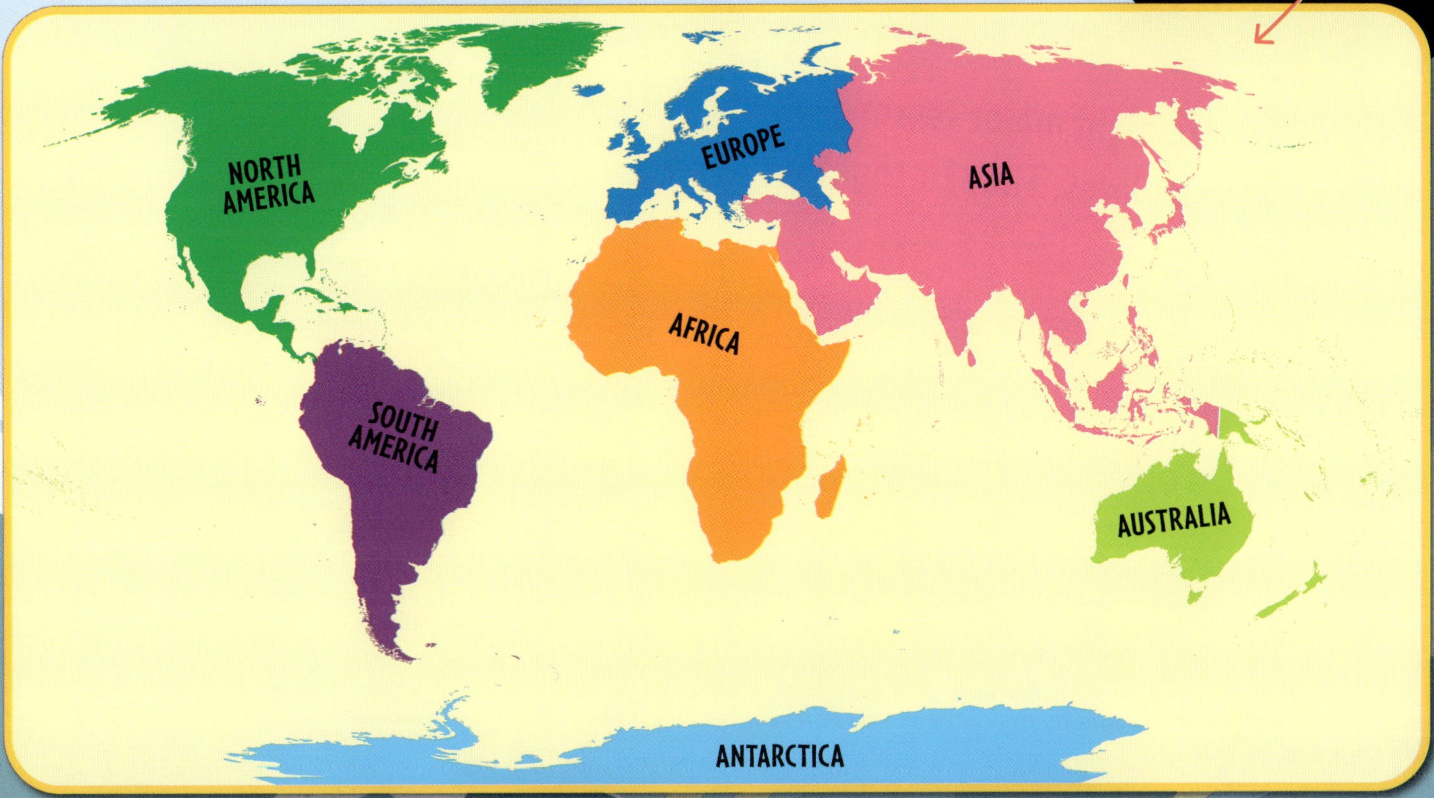

NORTH AMERICA
EUROPE
ASIA
AFRICA
SOUTH AMERICA
AUSTRALIA
ANTARCTICA

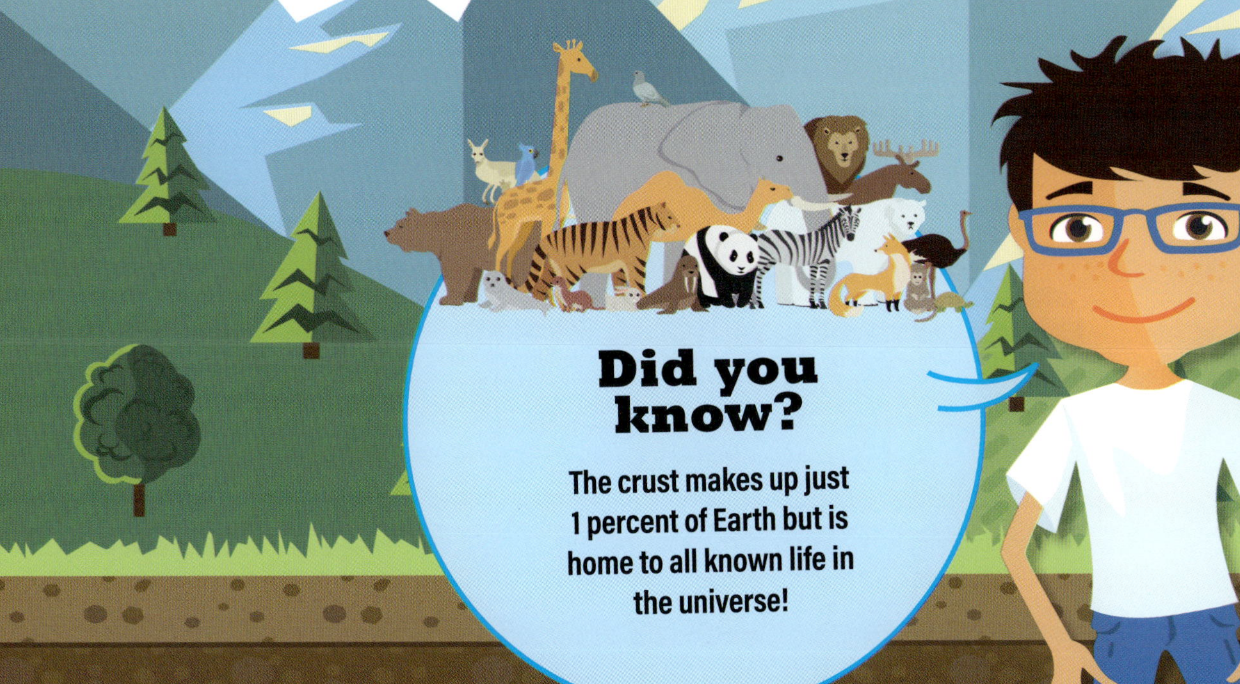

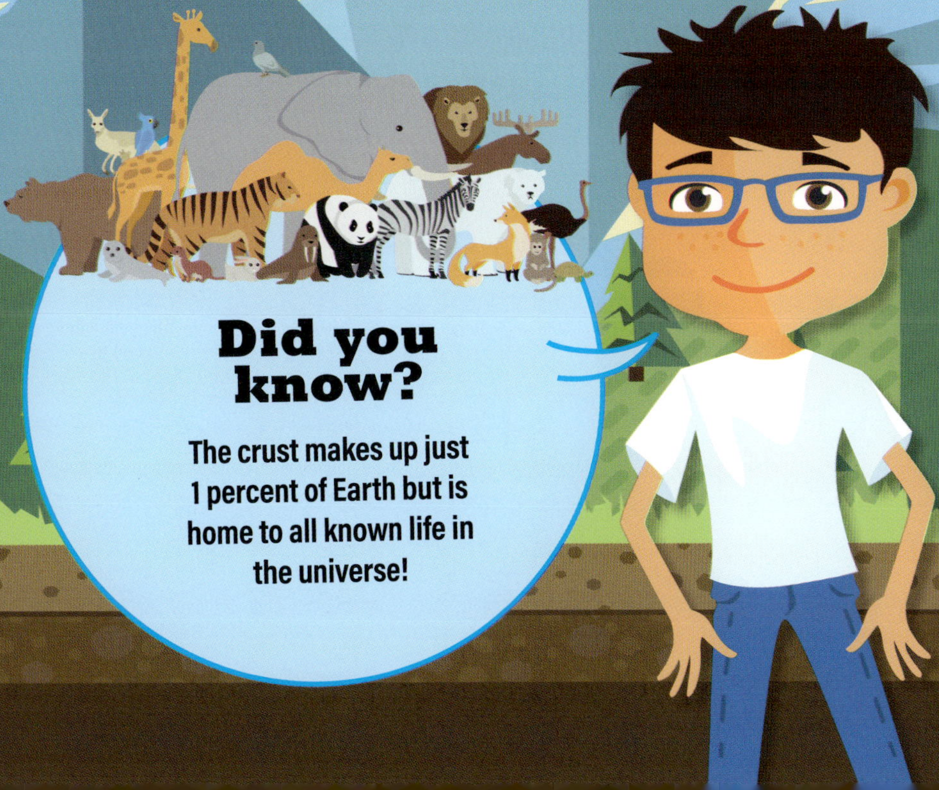

Did you know?

The crust makes up just 1 percent of Earth but is home to all known life in the universe!

TECTONIC PLATES

Earth's crust is split into huge pieces called tectonic plates.

There are eight major tectonic plates and many smaller tectonic plates. They fit together like a jigsaw puzzle.

Move it!

Tectonic plates lie on a layer of semi-molten rock in the mantle. The movement of rock in the mantle moves the tectonic plates on the surface.

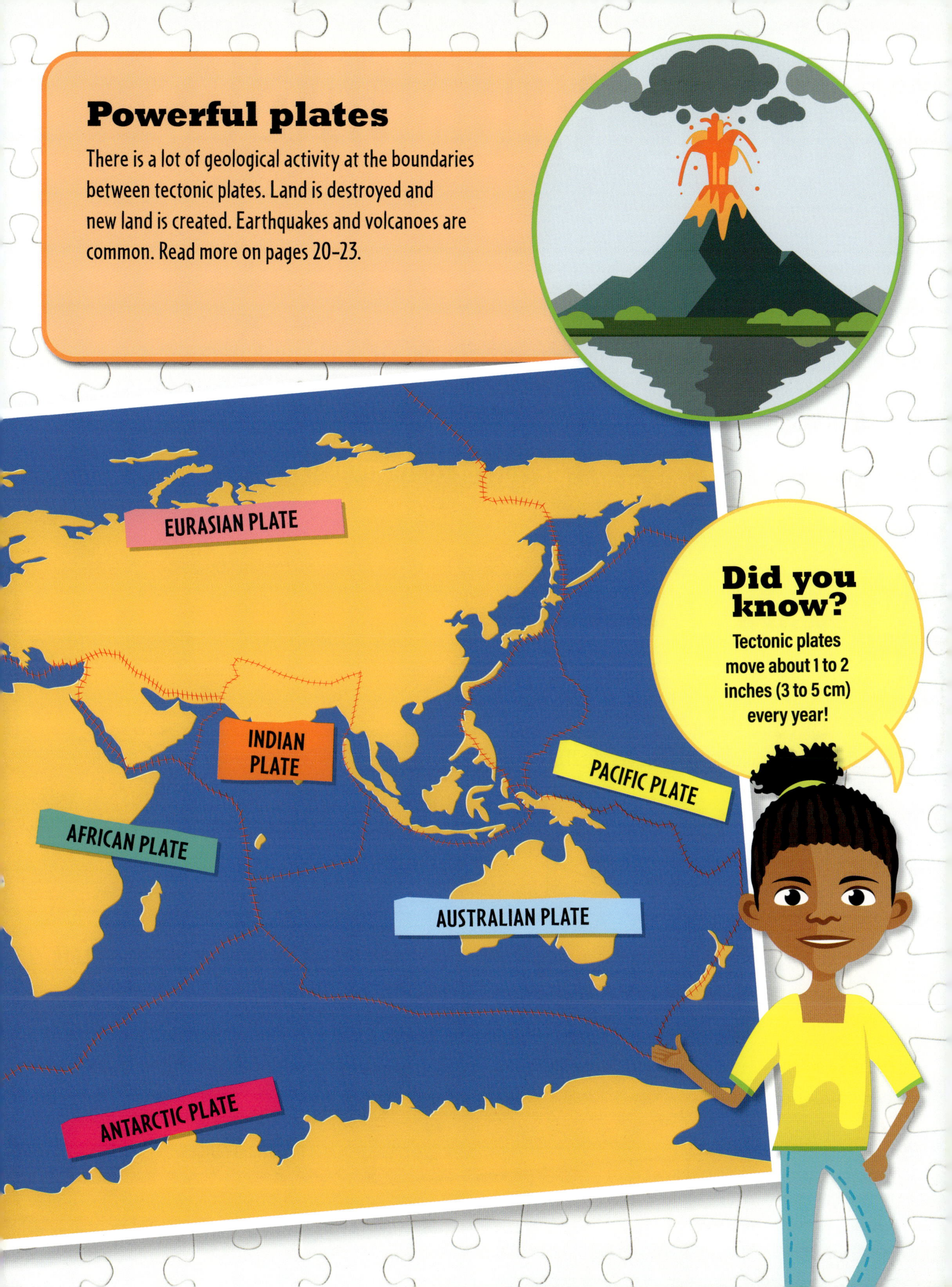

Powerful plates

There is a lot of geological activity at the boundaries between tectonic plates. Land is destroyed and new land is created. Earthquakes and volcanoes are common. Read more on pages 20–23.

Did you know?

Tectonic plates move about 1 to 2 inches (3 to 5 cm) every year!

PLATE BOUNDARIES

There are several different types of boundary where tectonic plates meet.

The type of boundary between the tectonic plates depends on whether the plates are moving towards each other, away from each other or past each other. It also depends on whether the plates are made of oceanic crust or continental crust.

Towards each other

When an oceanic plate meets a continental plate, the thin oceanic crust is pushed down under the continental crust. The oceanic crust melts under the continental crust and can create volcanoes (see pages 20-21).

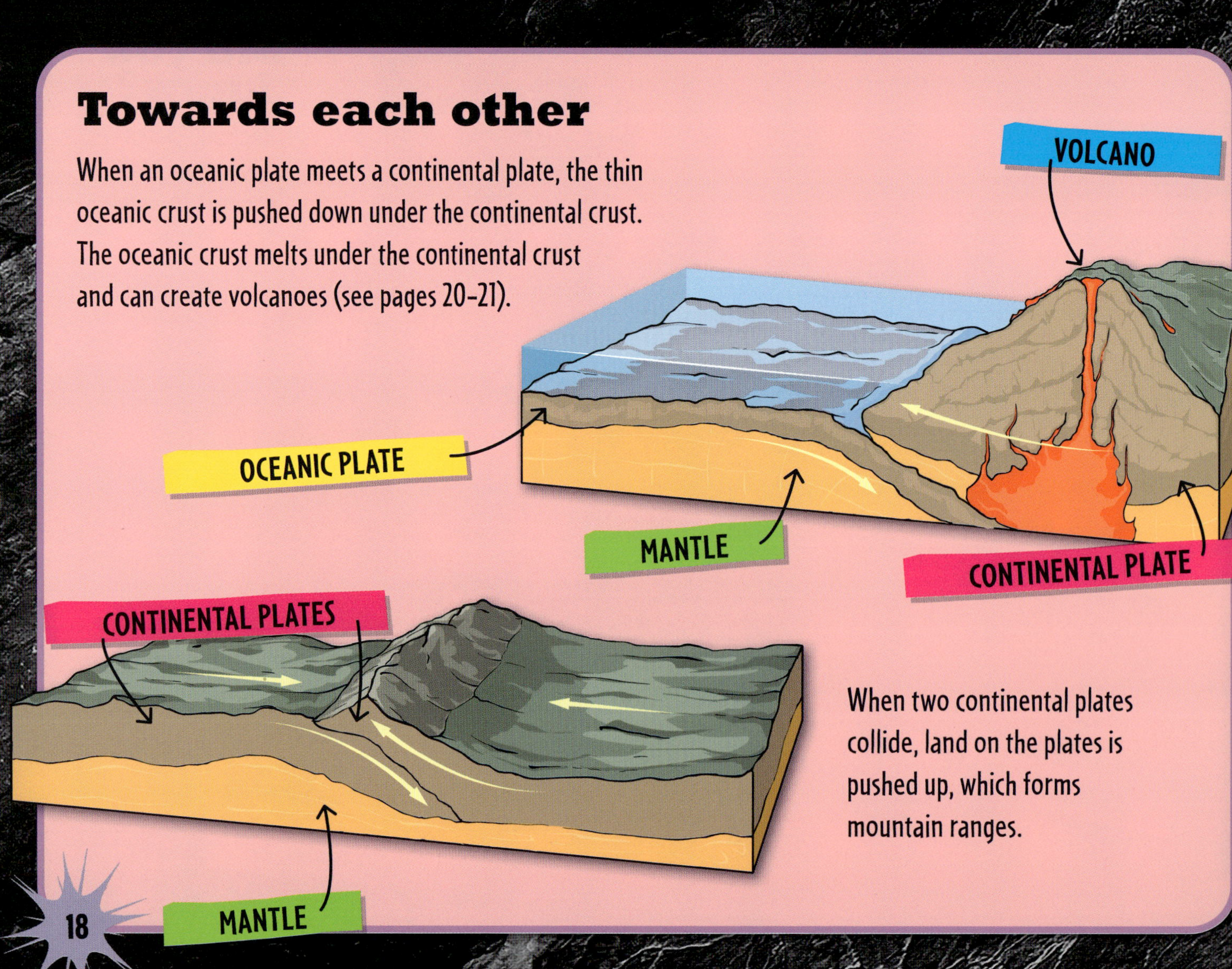

When two continental plates collide, land on the plates is pushed up, which forms mountain ranges.

Away from each other

If two oceanic plates move away from each other, magma from the mantle moves up into the gap between them. This magma cools to form new rock and new oceanic crust is formed.

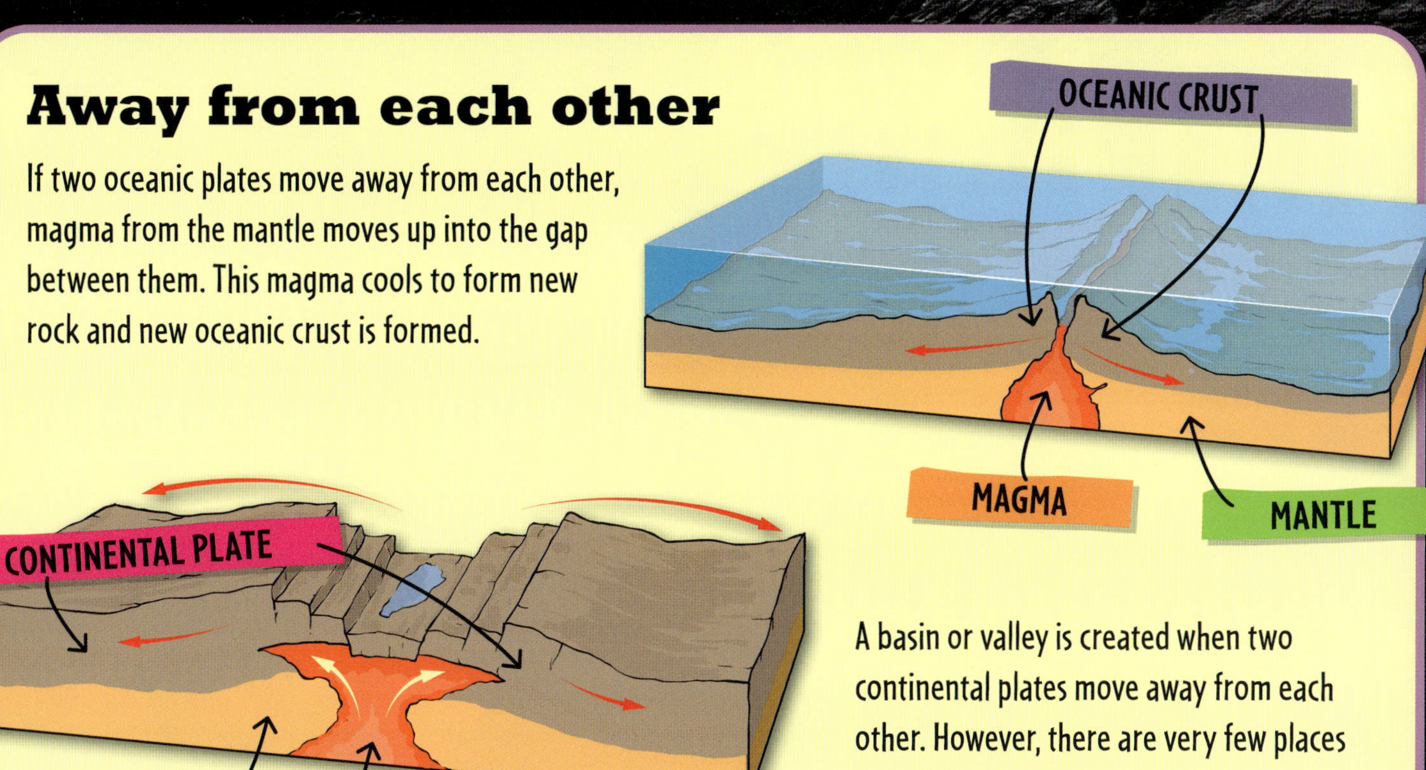

A basin or valley is created when two continental plates move away from each other. However, there are very few places where this happens.

Past each other

When tectonic plates slide past each other in opposite directions, or in the same direction but at different speeds, they can get stuck and friction builds up. This continues until the plates suddenly jolt past each other. This triggers an earthquake (see pages 22–23).

CONTINENTAL PLATE

MANTLE

It's a fact

Oceanic crust is much younger than continental crust because it is constantly being destroyed and created along plate boundaries. The oldest oceanic crust is only 270 million years old, while the oldest continental crust is over 4 billion years old!

VOLCANOES

Volcanoes are often found at the edges of tectonic plates.

A volcano is an opening in Earth's crust where gas and hot, molten rock come to the surface. Volcanoes often explode in dramatic eruptions!

Inside an active volcano

1 Molten rock (magma) builds up in the magma chamber.

2 Eventually, the magma chamber becomes so full that magma is forced out through an opening in the surface. Once magma reaches the surface, it is known as lava.

3 Lava, gas, and dust sometimes explode out into the air, creating a huge cloud.

Hot spots

Volcanoes are also found on hot spots. These are very hot areas of the mantle in the middle of tectonic plates. The islands of Hawaii were created by a hot spot in the Pacific tectonic plate.

4

Lava can also flow across the surface. When it cools down, it hardens into solid rock.

Did you know?

There are around 1,500 active volcanoes on Earth today!

PHOTO QUIZ!

This Roman town was famously destroyed by a volcano called Vesuvius in 79 CE. What was the name of the town? Answer on page 28.

EARTHQUAKES

Earthquakes are waves of vibrations that can be triggered by moving tectonic plates.

The ground shakes during an earthquake!

Plates under pressure

When tectonic plates slide past each other, they can become stuck. Pressure builds up until the plates suddenly slide past each other. This releases vibrations that are also known as an earthquake. The vibrations, or shockwaves, move across the land in every direction.

PLACE WHERE THE EARTHQUAKE BEGAN

EARTHQUAKE SHOCKWAVES

MOVING TECTONIC PLATES

Serious shockwaves

Shockwaves from an earthquake can be weak or very strong. The greater the shockwave, the more damage it can cause. Powerful earthquakes can knock over buildings and destroy roads and electrical cables. Earthquakes can also set off massive waves called tsunamis.

PHOTO QUIZ!

Earthquakes can make this happen. What is it called? Answer on page 28.

2-liter bottle

Make a tsunami in a bottle

Recreate the dramatic movement of a tsunami wave safely inside a bottle! You will need an empty, clear 2-liter bottle with a lid, clean gravel, water, and an adult to supervise.

1. Fill the empty bottle with a 2-inch (5 cm) layer of gravel.

2. Pour water on top of the gravel until the bottle is about one-quarter full. Put the lid on.

3. Carefully lay the bottle on its side. The gravel should create a small slope, like a coastline.

4. Hit the lid of the bottle with your hand once. This movement will create vibrations, like those in an earthquake.

5. Watch as the vibrations travel through the water and push it up on to the gravel.

This is exactly how a tsunami moves across the ocean and up on to the shore.

UNDERGROUD EXPLORATION

So far, humans have never explored or traveled beneath Earth's crust. However, there are many ways that we can learn about its other layers.

We know a lot about the structure of Earth without ever seeing it for ourselves!

We don't currently have the equipment to dig a deep enough hole or to withstand the conditions beneath the crust.

I'm going to get there, promise!

Surface science

Everything we know about the inner layers of our planet comes from data that geologists have gathered on the surface. For example, measuring how earthquake shockwaves move through Earth proved that the inner core is solid but the outer core is liquid. This is because shockwaves move differently through solid and liquid materials.

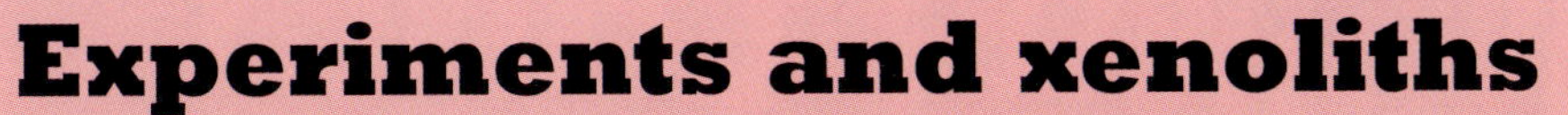

Experiments and xenoliths

Scientists can do experiments that recreate the conditions inside Earth to see how different rocks react. They also study xenoliths. These are rocks from deep inside the mantle that become trapped inside other rocks and brought to the surface. The rock around a xenolith protects it from being changed by the conditions in the mantle.

Did you know?

Scientists have also found xenoliths from outer space in meteorites that have landed on Earth!

OUR CHANGING PLANET

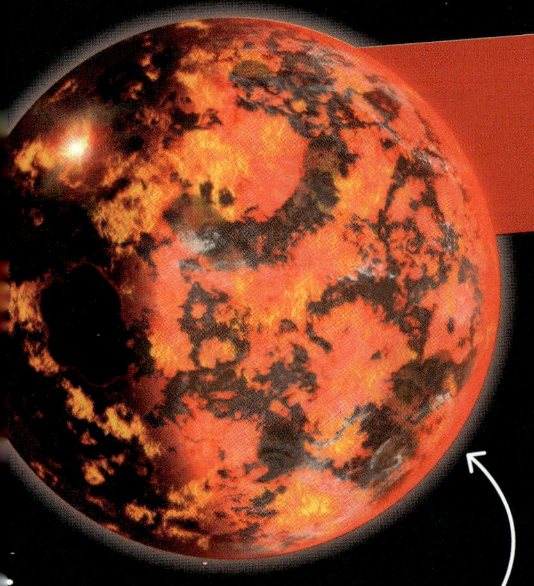

This is an artist's interpretation of what Earth might have looked like when it was mostly magma.

Earth hasn't always looked the same as it does today.

Earth is around 4.6 billion years old. It has changed a lot in that time!

Early days

At first, Earth was a hot, sticky ball of magma. Eventually, the heaviest materials—metals—sunk to the center and became the core. The mantle cooled and Earth formed a solid crust. Liquid water formed oceans on the surface.

On the move

The areas of land and sea on Earth's crust haven't always been the same. This is because of the movement of tectonic plates.

Just before the time of the dinosaurs, many of the continents that are separate today were joined together to make one large supercontinent.

During and after the time of the dinosaurs, the supercontinent split apart into separate pieces of land.

QUICK QUIZ!

The coastlines of these two continents fit together almost like a jigsaw! This is because they were both part of the same piece of land, which split in two. Which continents are they? Answer on page 28.

It's a fact

The movement of the land on Earth explains why fossils of a prehistoric coastal reptile called *Mesosaurus* have been found in Africa and South America, even though it couldn't cross the ocean!

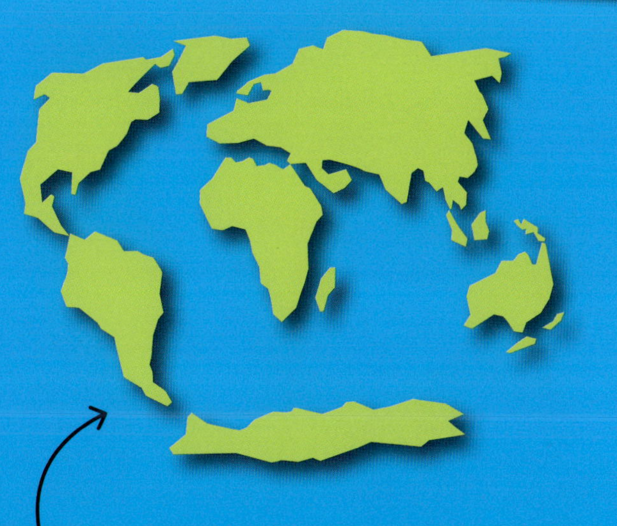

Over millions of years, the continents moved into the position they are in today. In the future, the land on Earth may look totally different again!

QUICK QUIZ ANSWERS

PAGE 7
Gold

PAGE 9
Saturn

PAGE 11
Near the North and South Poles

PAGE 21
Pompeii

PAGE 23
A landslide

PAGE 27
Africa and South America

NOW TEST YOUR KNOWLEDGE!

1 **Which of Earth's layers is the thickest?**

a. Crust

b. Outer core

c. Mantle

2 **Why does the iron in the inner core stay solid?**

a. High pressure

b. Low temperature

c. Other elements keep it liquid

3 **Which of Earth's layers creates the planet's magnetic field?**

a. Inner core

b. Outer core

c. Crust

4 **How much does a tectonic plate move each year?**

a. 0.04 to 0.08 inch (1 to 2 mm)

b. 1 to 2 inches (3 to 5 cm)

c. 20 to 23 feet (6 to 7 m)

ANSWERS ON PAGE 31

5 **What is a hot spot?**

a. An area of the crust where the sun shines a lot

b. The hottest part of Earth's core

c. A very hot area of the mantle in the middle of a tectonic plate

6 **When was all the land on Earth joined together to make one supercontinent?**

a. Just before the time of the dinosaurs

b. Just after the time of the dinosaurs

c. When the first humans walked on Earth

GLOSSARY

boundary – a line that divides two areas

continent – one of the seven main large areas of land on Earth

core – the central part of Earth's structure

crust – the outer layer of Earth

dense – containing a lot of matter in a small space

element – a substance that is only made of one thing and can't be broken down into smaller parts

igneous rock – rock that is formed from cooled magma

lava – hot molten rock above the ground

magma – hot molten rock under the ground

magnetic field – the area around a magnet or something magnetic that is affected by its magnetic force

mantle – the middle layer of Earth's structure

molten – melted

particle – a very small piece of something

prehistoric – from the time before there were written records of history

pressure – a force that pushes on things

sphere – a 3D circle

tectonic plate – a piece of Earth's crust

tsunami – a giant wave in the ocean

vibration – a quick, shaking movement

FURTHER READING

BOOKS

Bradley, Doug. *20 Things You Didn't Know About Geology*. Buffalo, NY: PowerKids Press, 2023.

Olson, Elsie. *Geology Lab: Explore Earth with Art & Activities*. Minneapolis, MN: Abdo Publishing, 2024.

Schuh, Mari C. *Earth: The Planet of Life*. Minneapolis, MN: Jump!, 2023.

WEBSITES

www.dkfindout.com/us/quiz/earth/test-yourself-on-structure-earth/
Test your knowledge of Earth's layers.

easyscienceforkids.com/all-about-volcanoes/
Discover more about volcanoes.

Answers: 1c, 2a, 3b, 4b, 5c, 6a

INDEX